METATRON

This is the Healing Book

D1674651

Front cover image courtesy of the Hubble Space telescope.

www.imetatron.com

Greetings! Welcome! I am Lord Metatron, the Angelic presence that encompasses the Universe. We bring you this second book with Joy, with Love, with Peace, with Power. Awakening you to the understanding of your Majestic presence. As individualised beings of God. In this incarnation for you, you understand the way that you have moved forward and you have learned many lessons and as lightworkers you have wanted to heal the world. When you first awoke this was the only thing that you wanted.

You must understand that the most powerful way to awaken the World is to awaken yourself fully, wholly and completely without judgement of anybody. Purifying your vessels, cleansing, partaking of pure food, exercising, praying, meditating, and being at your core centre that you embody God. That you *are* God and as God you can heal anything for you understand that everything is perfect and all around you Flowers, all around you is lifted up in your presence. This is the greatest goal of the lightworker.

The healing of all will happen. All must go through the lessons that they need for their soul but this Planet is accelerating in its ascension, is accelerating in its purification, is accelerating in its evolution and you are here to facilitate this Dear Ones. Understand the Power that you have. Cleanse, meditate, purify, pray. Be at one with yourself - be ready.

In this Book we will show you what you need to do in order to bring your vibration to the Point of purity that you may heal Mentally, Emotionally, Physically, Spiritually, and you may be Healers to One and All. Just being in your presence will be Healing, will be calming, will take you to the next level of understanding who you are. Do not judge, merely absorb the lesson. Be at one with Yourself, We Love you and we are here with you, guiding this, guiding you always and loving you always.

Over the course of this book we are going to infuse you with Intergalactic energies that you will be Glowing by the end of this book. If you approach it with humility you will learn the lesson, you will take these lessons on and you will Glow with Light, with Love, with healing, with Purity. We know each and every one of you that is reading this Book right now and we Love you all. Be at Peace, be ready, imbibe the Lessons that we give you and you will be jumping for Joy. You will be rejoicing in this understanding. We love you - you are ready. I am Archangel Metatron and I love you.

I am the Channel that Spirit used to bring this information down. It has been my great honour and privilege to be a part of this project.

I developed as a medium in a meditation circle years ago. I didn't know about ascension or any of the New Age stuff before I developed, but I always felt that there was something else in life that I should be doing.

Since learning how to channel, my life has become much better, and I am often astounded by the stuff that comes out. The process is simple - I go into a meditative state and I feel a great loving presence and hear a phrase repeated over and over. As soon as I hear the phrase, I let it repeat a few times so I know it is not just my inner dialogue, and then repeat it. After that I just keep on talking and sometimes can still be talking half an hour later.

This is all recorded and afterwards I transcribe it. This whole book was written this way, and it has been wonderful to feel the bliss that the high vibration brings. I have learned a lot from this whole process and my life is much better for it. I hope that reading this book brings you as much joy and understanding as it has done for me.

This is the second Book I have been asked to bring down for Metatron. The first is 'Metatron, this is the Clarion Call'. It is available on Amazon.

Best wishes,

Robbie Mackenzie

I am Archangel Metatron, I bring you the healing book. Following this instruction fully you will become a divine healer. This is the beginning of the Metatron tradition. I give this legacy to you. This begins an open energy, an open dialogue to your core energy, your source energy, your God-self, your Angelic presence. You must understand this illusion that you have created, how to transform it, how to subtly manipulate the energy for maximum health, for maximum vitality and for maximum joy. You all have this core energy dear ones. I am helping you transform, helping you open up to an understanding of your wider selves, that is all that healing is. I am bringing you to your at-one-ment with the Universe.

We start this journey with your mental body. For your understanding as individualised beings of your creation starts with your mental body. With your thoughts you make the World. You make the Universe. You have created all that is here in this three dimensional World. You are going to stop struggling. For it is in your struggle that you feel ill at ease with yourselves and with others. Coming to the centre point with your mental direction you will connect with everything. With your four-body system - Your mental body, your emotional body, your spiritual body and your physical body.

Peace, this is where the zero point of your source energy is. It is not good, nor bad, it is pure energy. Understanding the power of your thoughts will be to understand what you are about to create.

This is the first infusion of Metatronic energy

Be ready and be calm as you accept this energy within your vessel. You shall feel this. This is the first of the infusions I am giving you directly.

Be in a quiet calm place where you will not be disturbed. Sit comfortably. Put your hands into the prayer position and close your eyes. Regulate your breathing.

Accept this first transmission of light

This is your zero point energy. Feel this energy flowing through you

The pages of this book are being infused with this divine energy. This first exercise is very important. This first connection, Feel this energy for this sets the scene for your learning, for your attunement, for your understanding, for your awareness. This is the most important moment in this book. This is pulling together your four-body system. Allowing you to be ready for all that is to come.

It is important that once you have read through this that you sit and you allow my energies to come through you, infusing you. This is raising your vibration. This energetic connection will connect you to all others that are reading this book. Infusing you with Metatronic energy.

Breathe and accept this light. Receive this purity - receive this truth

As you feel this infusion your clarity is going to expand more and more, your visions, your dreams and great expansion. Accept this energy, accept this flow, you are being brought into your mastery. Allow yourself to get lost in this energy. Do not worry about the timeline. Let all worries go, relax into the flow. You are at the perfect point in your spiritual evolution to accept this energy. This is your first initiation.

In order to become clear you must put yourselves in the hands of the heavenly hierarchy, for we are overseeing humanities transition and evolution, your spiritual evolution, mental, emotional and physical evolution. You are changing dear ones and the higher vibration babies you are giving birth to, many are coming in already switched on, already opened up. All the old paradigms are breaking down and you are walking into a brave new World. We love you and we are here with you. You will become clear, clear individuals.

These transmissions of light that we give you must be fully integrated in your life. As you walk forward in society you do not have to preach at all. You have to embrace and embody these new energies, these vibrant energies of healing and you will become healed, you will become whole, you will become holy, this is what holy means, it means whole, complete and integrated Human beings - the next stage of your evolution. The more you heal, the more you awaken, the more telepathic you become and your mental body will expand more and more as you connect to all the individuals surrounding you that are of a higher vibration. This is linking you to the worldwide grid on your Planet. The more you open up to this the more you will be freed. Your old ways of acting will drop off as you embody the bliss, as you embody the love, as you embody the truth of spirit.

The heavenly hierarchy and the Galactic council are overseeing this whole endeavour. We are giving you exactly what you need at this time dear ones. Do not over complicate things in your minds; rather see things for what they are. Face and embrace your filter system so that you may clear it from all the negatives that were given you from birth to your awakening. All the negative attitudes, all the things that happened to you that made you feel off centre that made you feel unworthy, that made you feel different. You are the next stage of humanity. You are the next stage of the evolution of mankind. Therefore appreciate yourself. Face your filter system within your mental body. Understand what you have been given in your religious, societal and familial conditions. Review what you have been given, review old prejudices, review old biases. For in dealing with your mental body, in dealing with your filter system, in clearing this away, taking away the debris, you are in effect decanting yourself so that there is no sediment left. This is leading to a clear mind. As we give you the transmissions of light, as you open up to this purity, we subtly change your consciousness so that you are not affected anymore by the old patterns and belief systems that have held you down and have stopped you from being free. This work with this book in tandem with you opening your merkaba will free you to do be and have whatever you want and will allow you in the presence of others to help them clear their mental bodies.

We encourage you to write down your conditions. For you to review all that has happened to you in this incarnation. For you to face it and for you to clear it so that you may move onto the next stage and be cleared human beings.

We deal with your mental body first because this is the point at which you create your reality. This is the point at which your mighty imagination brings you in tandem with your level of vibration, what you create. The law of attraction is much misunderstood and it is true that with your thoughts you create the World however the reality you experience is dependant upon your level of vibration for how quickly you manifest. For at a lower vibration you are subject to other sentient beings vibration and creation. When your mental body is clear and when you have raised your vibration you can create whatever you want. When you understand this sliding scale of creation you will understand why when you have tried to put the law of attraction into action you have wondered why it has not worked for you were thinking the right things but you were not believing fully that it would happen and you did not raise your vibration to the point of bliss. When you raise your vibration to the zero point of bliss things are created very quickly in your reality. This is an important point to ponder. For when you understand this and when you really want to create the reality that *you* want to have you will put in the effort. Not only to create with your mind but to be in the centre point of bliss. For it is this love, it is this bliss that is the powerhouse of your creation. This is the key to your mastery; this is the key to you transforming everything with your mental body. This is the key to you healing completely and this is the key to you healing others.

As you come to stillness, as you clear your mind, you will understand that everything is a reflection of your consciousness, of your imagination. Everything that has ever been and everything that will ever be is a reflection of your imagination, of your consciousness. All the different traditions, religious and spiritual traditions are all true, within their own paradigm of understanding. But understand that this is your imagination and your imagination is very powerful as you create this three dimensional reality. This is a holographic projection of your imagination. The collective holographic presentation that we have made as a collective is very real and what you create within this holographic representation once you still your mind will be up to you. Coming to a point of complete non judgement, coming to a point of complete understanding of your creational abilities is coming to the understanding of your healing abilities within this paradigm of creation.

Once you clear your mind, once you clear your filter system, once you work in tandem with your mental, emotional, spiritual and physical bodies you will be in the place of the peace that passes understanding. This is the place of no mind. This encompasses all of creation. It is the everything and it is the nothing. It is, as above, so below. It is the point where you are the centre. You are the seed, you are the action and you are the fruit. This is the most powerful form of awareness, this is expanded consciousness and this encompasses all time and all of creation. In your individualised vessels when you come to this understanding, when you experience it, you are ready to create and from this place you are ready to heal.

From the limited perspective of disease in human kind you look upon disease and you see the suffering that it entails but you persist with the structures of thought that have created this disease and allow yourself to be stuck in a negative paradigm of experience. This will completely change when you come to your zero point.

Relax; be open and ready to receive the next download of energy

This download will help clear the visions of your linear past that have stood in your way from being at peace. Sit quietly, ready, close your eyes and sit in a comfortable position. Feel the energy come upon you. All the visions that you are going to see in your third eye, allow them to flow through you, take a step back from them and watch as a spectator as if you are in a cinema, watch. This is the overview of energy and it is transforming you. Sit, be quiet, and allow me to give you exactly what you need. This is tailor made for your individualised vessel. Relax; allow it to come through you.

Be open and receive

We give you these downloads to bring you into alignment with your divine self. For in your divine state you are completely healed, completely pure, completely at your centre. These downloads are more of an opening up. It is you coming into your divine focus, it is coming into your divine truth, it is coming into the understanding of you as your God self.

Your understanding of healing is going to expand and extend. For once you understand that as a divine healer the greatest work that you can do for others is to work on your self. Your mental, emotional, spiritual and physical bodies are very important. Your medicine concentrates on the physical body. We will leave this body till later in this book. This is very important for you to understand what the make up of your physical vessel is. You understand it as an upgrade as you upgrade your computers and your operating system becomes more efficient and you can access more technology. With these downloads you will have all the software that you will ever need to heal yourself and to heal others. To bring them into alignment with their divine selves. Once you assimilate these concepts you will be open more and more to what is happening within your vessels.

This next download we give you is to descend the bliss into your four-body system. It is important that once you have had this download that you drink water. This transformation overall completely, if you follow this book to the word, will happen gradually over a seven week period. You will feel yourself coming more into alignment with peace, with the purity of your own self.

Relax; be open and receive this download

This is the bliss download. This is the centre place of your heart chakra. Allow and absorb this. Feel this awakening within you. The centre point of your heart opening up, breathe, allow. This is the most important download. From this place, centred within your heart you are able to access all the healing for your four-body system. This is the bridge to the emotional body. This is the download that will affect you on the most profound level. That will expand out to your whole physical experience. For this place of love is the greatest healing place of all. Allow the tears to flow as this download affects you. Allow yourself to be immersed in this divine centre, this divine love. Breathe in this peace. Breathe in this love.

The healing energy that you emit when you come into your power and the peace that you will embody will be very calming and very peaceful, very healing for people and you will come to peace with yourself completely. As a diviner healer understand that you are merely a channel for spirit. You are a channel for the healing energies. So as you let go fully more and more to the Metatronic healing power you are healed more and more. You are given more and more bliss, you are opened up to a whole new world of peace, a whole new world of power.

This three dimensional world is made through your merkaba, was created through the power of the divine energy. As you connect more and more to the Metatron, as you connect more and more to my healing power, you begin to embody the Metatron. This is something that you can all do dear ones. This is not putting Metatron above you or you below Metatron. This is your higher self, this is the truth of the Universe and is a point of your consciousness that when you reach you begin to embody these powerful healing energies, these powerful creational energies. You rise above your lower selves and you open to divine bliss. This is you giving you the gift; this is you giving you this peace. The next stage of your awareness, the next stage of your powerful healing is to come to this understanding.

We encourage your purification, we encourage you eating pure food, drinking lots of water, meditating regularly and accepting the downloads of Metatronic energy. We encourage you to do this regularly and as you clear your bodies, mental, emotional, physical and spiritual your understanding of what you are here to do, of what your divine mission is. Of the bliss that pulls you in the direction of your own excitement from moment to moment will become more obvious and instead of being a slave to other peoples opinions, different patterns from your Parents, from your society, from your religious backgrounds will fade away as you come into your power and you appreciate your worthiness. This is you coming into your healed selves; this is you coming into your whole selves as you walk the holy path. As a divine awake healer, a divine awake individual your life will become more exciting and yet more peaceful. Moment to moment you will heal everyone that is around you.

This next download is to open up and awaken your divine Kundalini, your divine sexuality. This will take away the shame, the negativity and all detrimental effects that have been put upon your consciousness through society, through religion, through your familial understanding. This will help clear your filter system and bring you into your divine God/Goddess selves that you may embrace your sexuality and that your kundalini will rise through your base chakra up to your crown chakra. And you may feel the flow of energy and not waste it in disrespect or negativity and will help you honour this for yourself and for all others that you come into contact with in a sexual way.

Your sexuality is a gift from the Universe, it is a wonderful and powerful healing tool when understood correctly to help Mankind free themselves from the bondage that they have been under for millennia. All the abuse that has happened, all the pain that has been inflicted has been because as a species you have manipulated and misled each other to the belief that your sexual connections are wrong, are unholy, are sinful, even believing that sin is what created you in the physical. This is not the truth dear ones, you are sexual beings and once you embrace this within your vessels no matter what your orientation is, once you embrace yourself you will help the world be more at ease with themselves and all the pain that has come out of these negative concepts will be released.

As you begin to understand the power of your sexual energy as it flows through your body instead of merely understanding it from a physical perspective of genital excitement. When you understand and honour this your Kundalini will be free to flow and your power to heal others, to free others, to awaken others and to embody the bliss of your own sexuality will multiply your powers of healing.

This download is very powerful

Be open to receive this

As we give you this download we open up your base chakra, fully open. Be at peace with everything that happens around your genitals at this time. Do not be in fear - embrace it. As this download continues the energy will rise up through your sacral chakra, through your solar plexus to your heart. Your expanded awareness from your heart to your genitals will be fully accepted as you embrace this download. From your heart the energy rises through your throat chakra, through your third eye, through your crown chakra connecting you to all the soul mates that you are meant to be in contact with that will honour your sexuality that will respect your vessel and will respect your mission and what you are here for.

There is an excitement surrounding this download such as you have never experienced before opening your kundalini and this flow awakens you to the new humanity of love and trust and divine sexuality. With this download we increase the power. This download is deeply connected to your emotional body. This will take down all the barriers and will allow you to be in a flow state. Breathe deeply and embrace what is going on in your vessel just now.

Open to receive this download fully

We bring you the light; we bring you the full quotient of the light within your vessel. As you open up as divine healers you will feel this light come upon you more and more until you fully embody the light. This healing book is a book for your healing personally, for you healing others in their four-body system and it is also a book for healing the World, for becoming the beacons of healing, of light, of the truth of your core centre. As you embody this light more and more in tandem with you opening your merkaba you walk forward as masters of light, of love. And the reward for this is pure bliss. You are creating new paradigms on this Earth. Clearing the complications of negative dogma and doctrine from the past. Changing the consciousness of the World. The balance of light has already tipped in the favour of the new opening consciousness. In your linear understanding of time this happened at the Winter solstice in 2012. It is a subtle change but the balance has been tipped towards an opening awakening truthful   understanding   with   Humanities   curiosity   and acceptance and feeling that good things are ahead for your species.

All that would entrap and ensnare Mankind are a small minority and it has seemed in the past as if they were the Elephant and the people striving for truth were a gnat on their back. But the truth is that the people who would enslave mankind in all the different ways that they are trying to right now in your linear time are beginning to understand that they are the gnat and you are the Elephant.

All you have to do as divine healers is bathe in your own bliss and create the paradigm that you want for your own life. Letting go of all negativity. Not feeding into the concept of the big bad wolf or the Illuminati, entrapping you and enslaving mankind.

This next download we give you is for this Global transformation as divine healers, as divine lightworkers. This download will open up your compassion towards those that will try to enslave mankind. So that there is no opposition, that there is no duality. This will help raise them to their highest good and that the power they hold and resources that they have may be used for the good of Mankind to bring this Planet into a Utopia. For this is where you are headed dear ones. You are moving forward in the right direction. This download will help this greatly. It will clear away all fear of these people that do not have the collectives good at heart.

Be open and receive this download

As you assimilate these Galactic energies your whole body will start to tingle. Your whole body will start to vibrate with excitement at the higher resonance; the higher vibration and you will begin to see things changing in your own lives, the lives of those around you and the vibration of the World in general. You are becoming Galactic citizens. This book will help bridge the gap between you and the Galactic council and will allow you to feel connected to the many different beings all over the Universe that sit in the Galactic council. And will allow you to feel comfortable within this new paradigm of understanding that is coming upon your vessels.

You have made many leaps and bounds in your consciousness over the last hundred years. Your transportation has changed gradually. Your communication has changed gradually. And in this new millennia, in your linear understanding of time your transportation and communication is changing even more rapidly. When you master your merkabas you will understand that you can go wherever you want in the Universe with your consciousness and as you open up with the help of this book your communication will expand telepathically and you will understand the different levels of vibration that are on your Planet at the moment. You are complete within your vessels. This is one of the most healing concepts that you will come to the understanding of. That there is nothing inherently wrong with you and though things may seem faulty within your vessels from time to time. Everything can be healed completely, totally and unequivocally. With this book, with these downloads and a fully open merkaba and with the transformation of consciousness. A complete and unequivocal healing will occur.

While one is suffering on your Earth plane all are suffering. But this is just a stage of your consciousness. And for you to bring this World into the physical Utopia that it will become you must realize and visualise this as already here.

Grounding yourself is important as these Galactic energies come upon you. As you open up and as you move forward into your Galactic citizenship, as you fully heal these vessels you spread the understanding and you spread the awareness everything will become apparent as the bliss descends upon you. And as you open up your vessels you will start to see things from a clearer perspective. Fear will no longer be in the equation, as you will understand you are eternal beings, ever evolving, ever changing.

You have been at a plateau stage for some time. Now is the time for you to go to the next level, for you to embrace the capabilities of your individual vessels. The limitations that have been put upon you by society, by your family structures and by those who would hold you down in this society are being taken off. You are being opened up so you can fly dear ones. All the joy that you can embody is yours for the taking.

Never before has your Planet been able to communicate the way that it can do now and as your communication moves forward more telepathically you will be able to treat with compassion those who are not ready for this upgrade and you will be drawn to those who will help you fulfil your missions. For those who are in a lower vibration consciousness are individualised in their effectiveness. Those who are opening up to the new consciousness are unified and connected in the Christ grid. Are open to the guidance and the joining together which is a multiplication of your individual power. Not only will you feel more powerful but you will also see the evidence of this throughout humanity.

Grounding yourself mentally, emotionally, physically and spiritually is very important. Your visualisations will become much more powerful as you open up the capabilities within your mental body.

This next download is for you to ground fully into Gaia, your Mother Earth and for you to open up and connect fully with your Galactic tribe. As you accept this download you will feel the energy going from your heart to the centre of Earth. You will feel all the love going to Mother Earth, right to the centre. She is alive with consciousness and she loves you. As all this energy goes down to Mother Earth from your heart chakra it also goes up to the all that is, to everything else in your physical dimensions.

This download is an upgrade which will make all your endeavours much more successful. Will help you embrace everything that is going on within your vessel and will help you embrace the next stages as the downloads become much more powerful.

Be open and receive this download

Once this is assimilated fully within your vessel your acceptance will be complete and you will be open to the fireworks that will start to emanate from your body in an energetic fashion. This download anchors you fully for your Galactic mission. Once you have read through this, drink some water, get into prayer position and allow.

This is the halfway point and after this download is complete the intensity will multiply. Your bliss will multiply and your understanding of reality will be changed forever.

Be open and receive this upgrade

From here on in you will only be able to read past this point and fully assimilate the information in the downloads after you have fully integrated the first downloads that have happened so far. Understand dear ones, this book is an initiation for you to become fully open and integrated Human beings with your DNA fully opened, your aura clear, your filter system cleared, your Kundalini ignited, awakened and raised with your openness to walk into a whole new world and fully embrace your potential.

When we say you are becoming clear we mean that all falsehood is disappearing as you come into your natural selves, as you flower as individuals. As your higher self becomes your lower self, as you become your source energy, as the essence of you opens up you become more whole, complete and clear from all the lies that you have been told and all the manipulations and subversions of the truth fade away. You come into your confidence as embodiments of love. For that is the truth of your being, it is no more complicated than this dear ones, you are love, this is your source.

As you join together with the people who you love in this incarnation you are joining with people who remind you of your true self. But the truth is this is all an illusion dear ones. All are love at their core and so the more clear you become the more you see this within others and the more you see this within others the more it affects the vibration of the World. For as you do to one you do to all. As you do to another you do to yourself. So the benefit of becoming clear has a ripple effect for the rest of the World. The most important thing within your experience is that you come to this understanding yourself as an individualised being. From this place of bliss, from this place of understanding, from this place of peace all healing becomes very effective. Those who you will heal as a divine healer do not have to understand these concepts in order to be affected by your higher vibration.

The next part of this book is going to concentrate on your physical vessel and give you the tools as divine healers to be able to affect healings that will heal the individuals that you will be consciously laying your hands upon. In order to heal others effectively you must begin with yourself and feel the sensations of healing that come through your body for yourself.

This next exercise requires your physical participation

Sit in a comfortable place, on the floor would be preferable, on a cushion so that you are comfortable.

Sit with your back straight

Put your feet together, bending your knees so your soles are touching and your legs apart

Relax

Put your hands over your heart

This is a transmission of light codes for healing

Stage one – For healing yourself

Regulate your breathing

Allow these light codes to come through you

Individuals have their own light codes therefore in this place open your mind and allow these light codes to come upon you.

I am transmitting this directly to you for stage one of physical healing.

Breathe and embrace this

As you absorb the light codes take your hands from your heart and place them on your feet

For each individual there will be a different sensation. Embrace your own. You are like snowflakes dear ones, all individual merkabas and so the experience of this will be different for all.

Embrace the tingling sensations.

Move your hands to your calves

Feel the energy that is being encoded into your physical vessel right now.

Move your hands to your knees

You are building and anchoring your lightbody and healing on a cellular level

Move your hands to your thighs

As you feel the power of this healing keep moving your hands through your chakras.

First to your base chakra

Then to your sacral chakra

To your solar plexus

And to your heart

Remain at your heart now as the rest of the download is encoded upon you

Your higher three chakras are open and flowing all the information through to your heart chakra. Your lightbody is being fully rebuilt, your cellular memory is being restored and your body is being replenished.

Your breath is being regulated now

Metatrons cube is fully opening up in your heart

You are at the centre point of creation

You are the zero point

This evolutionary step is a conscious one. As you open up more and more your physical vessels will feel the lightness of being that comes from being fully open in your four body system. So much has weighed you down in this incarnation and so much is weighing others down. As you come to this lightness of being do not be afraid. Allow the energy to flow through you. You will take away the heaviness from others just by being in their presence and as you give them a formal healing, when you lay your hands upon them the codes of light will be transmitted from your hands. You are being lit up dear ones, freed completely.

This awakening is happening all over the Globe to differing degrees and as you embrace your mission you further accelerate everybody's growth.

Stage two in the physical healing process

Transmitting the codes of light

It has to be a cooperation dear ones for there has to be an acceptance within your vessels. If people wish to experience pain, suffering and disease for their soul journey it is not your place to affect a healing. This is a healing statement within itself for when you understand that everything is perfect and the growth of the universe is happening in complete divine timing, these experiences will benefit you greatly.

As you connect with another individual physically. Sit together, facing each other in a comfortable position. Place each other's right hand flat on each other's left hand.

Feel the flow of energy connect you

Feel your breath synchronising

Feel your Merkabas synching

At your hearts see Metatrons cube

Spinning in sync

Allow the download of energy

Allow the person to lie down in a comfortable position. Always asking for permission.

—

Place your hands at the person's feet

Allow the transmission of the codes of light to begin

I will guide you from this point as you intuitively move from the feet to the calves, to the thighs, to the side of the buttocks with both hands. Moving through all chakras till you get to the Crown chakra. When you are at the Crown chakra the greatest download will begin.

Allow the energy to flow through you

At this point you may feel all the ailments that the person you are healing is feeling. Allow yourself to absorb this and it will dissipate.

Advise the person to drink lots of water and to not eat any animal products, preferably indefinitely but for an effective healing for at least 48 hours.

You do not have to try to affect a healing. You are being a channel for this energy. All you have to do is allow.

As divine healers you must consider your nutrition. What you put in your body is very important. Within your species more than half of your diseases are caused by what you eat. Eating other sentient beings is not good for your vibration for many different reasons. You absorb the vibration from the animal on several different levels. The final energy of fear that these animals experience in feeling and understanding that they are going to their death is absorbed in their cellular memory. You cannot cook this vibration out. Although you can cook out a lot of the damaging things that would harm your body immediately through cooking you cannot cook out the vibration of the animal. Not only this final time before slaughter that is embedded in their consciousness are you imbibing but you are also taking on the nature of the animals that you are eating. This is not good for your vibration. It is confusing to your vessels and is part of the reason why you as a species have not come to peace. Without considering this, without accepting responsibility for what you are taking into your vessel you will not be able to rise to the highest vibration of your healing capabilities. Once you do you will see a marked difference in the clarity of your mind, in your vibration, in your four-body system. Giving up animal products does not only heal your vessel and help you become a more effective healer but it helps the world and helps break down the systems that are in place right now that are forcing a fear vibration over the whole of humanity. Not only this but in giving up animal products you will be helping the world towards economic freedom. This is the most important thing as divine healers that you will actively do to heal yourselves, to heal others and to heal the planet, Do not take this point lightly for the majority of things that need healed will be healed by this simple act once it is embraced by the whole of humanity. This is where your species are heading as you understand the nature of disease and you make the commitment to **really** heal the world, to **really** heal others and to **really** heal yourself. This is not a point that can be ignored. As you begin to embrace a plant based diet your vibration will raise rapidly. The majority of sensitive's that are at this point in this book already understand this but for the ones who have not do not fool yourselves into believing that this does not matter and that you can heal effectively whilst embracing the suffering of other sentient beings. Things are changing rapidly dear ones. Commit yourself to this process.

Be at peace with yourself as you embrace the many different sentient beings from all over the Universe that are surrounding your planet right now. Many different species that have been around for millennia that have been around for billions of years, that evolved long before you did and that have been watching you with great interest. The older the civilisation the more benevolent they are and there are many ancient civilisations that are connecting now to your consciousness, helping you telepathically, helping you move into your power, helping you embrace your peace, giving you technology and showing you the different options for your species to move forward.

Part of the transformation of consciousness is understanding that you have these beautiful benevolent souls as allies and the ones that are here on a healing mission only wish to help you see how you can bring effective healing into your lives and how you can develop as a species in connection with the different realms, the different dimensions, the different planetary resources that you have at your fingertips but have not been at a sufficient space within your consciousness to be able to utilise this or even grasp these concepts.

The linear time in your species evolution has arrived and there is a sufficient amount of like-minded souls in your species ready to embrace this.

Embracing your metatronic energy is embracing the core of the Universe and bringing you into sufficient autonomy as sovereign beings of light to understand that you have the power within you to connect and that you are ready to understand your true nature. We are giving you the blessing of the understanding of your interconnected interdependence with all living beings from all over this Universe and also the connection to the different dimensions that will benefit you as you evolve into oneness as a species.

This next download is a communications package. A tuning dial if you will. To give you the capabilities to connect directly, each and every one of you, not only with souls who are physically incarnated in this universe but souls from many different universes in many different dimensions. This is a download to awaken your antenna if you will and this download will sensitize your whole being.

Relax and embrace this download

This tuning dial will connect you directly to the Galactic council. Will show you the template for humanities evolution and give you the confidence to know you are not alone in the universe and that the majority of extra terrestrial civilisations wish to embrace you now as a species as your quarantine is over and you are being embraced with open arms by the many different cultures and civilisations that look upon you very fondly from all over the universe. Your lights are shining dear ones.

Do not fear these connections, they are benevolent and your lives will be enriched from these connections. Your technology will take leaps and bounds and as your scientists and engineers open up their antenna the world will be healed more rapidly and you will understand what true harmony is.

Your understanding of time is changing. As you fully sit in the centre place at the zero point within your Metatrons cube in your merkaba you open up to the understanding of time being always one. When you fully assimilate this concept your experience of life will change dramatically as you understand you can affect the World around you and you can access all the technology from the future and correct the mistakes of the past as you see it in your understanding. This is a very healing thing for you understand that you create yourself from moment to moment and that everything in the universe is morphable. As a creator being fully in your mastery you create the reality that you want to have.

The downloads we have given you so far have affected your four body system and have helped you within the paradigm of existence that you have created as a species. This next download will bring you fully into the zero point; will give you complete access to the zero point energy that you may experience 'no time' and will open up your control of your merkaba so that you can control it more efficiently. Understand that these downloads are to be used in tandem with you opening your merkaba.

Regulate your breathing as you accept this download

Hold at the bottom of your breath

Hold at the top of your breath

As you experience this download you will be given symbols that will appear like yantras in your third eye as you fully embrace this download.

Concentrate on these symbols

Concentrate on your breath

Your intent is very important as a healer. As you heal peoples four body systems what is being healed is not always very apparent. Being in your presence after you have assimilated all these downloads fully and completely and once you have opened your merkaba with you accepting the place within you that is completely healing you will heal people on many different levels. The emotional body will be balanced out while in your company.

The old paradigm of friendship will drop as you come into more mastery of your energy. Others will rise to you and seek your company. You must be discerning in this for as healers and lightworkers you are here yes to heal them and to help them but you must understand that while they are using you as their source they are not embodying their own power. So you are here first to help them plug in and to stay separate. This is showing unconditional love, this is empowering. Bringing them into their mastery without having your energy leached. This is a very important point we mention right now. As you have reached this point in the book you are ready to open fully and assimilate all the Galactic energies that we are going to put through you, that you are going to start to flow with for the rest of your life. As your life becomes a symphony of joy, of peace, of tranquillity, of excitement and it does not matter what others are doing. You must not concentrate on what others are doing or judging them at all for this is your creation now. You are in the centre flow, you are connecting to the Galactic council and you are connecting to all the other beings who are in their sovereign state and as you in your sovereign state are more compassionate to the plight of others yes this is true however in understanding to help them heal, to help them come into their sovereignty is to allow them to make their mistakes, to allow them to suffer.

This is your magic carpet ride; this is you embracing the next stage of your consciousness, the next stage of your joy. As divine healers you are not here to fix any situation, you are here to create new situations, create a whole new paradigm of existence.

The more you move into your complete mastery, your complete sovereignty the more you will find that people will be healed just by touching you and by you touching them. Your distance healing will become much more effective. You will recognize other healers on their path immediately.

In this next part of the book we are connecting you to the divine healers all over the Universe. You are part of a team now and all the healers who have passed the ring pass not will help facilitate you in your healing endeavours. It does not matter where they are from for they understand that we are all one. Some of these beings may be from trillions of light years away. As you connect to more advanced healers, advanced civilisations that are nowhere near this Universe physically you connect to them telepathically, instantaneously.

This next connection is an active download and meditation in one. For this download/meditation you must stand with your legs slightly apart and your hands crossed over your heart chakra. Moving your hips from side to side and swivelling them around clockwise and anti clockwise.

Regulate your breathing

Keep moving your hips round and round

Holding onto your heart chakra

Now spread your arms out to your side

Tilt your head back - still swivelling your hips

Regulate your breathing

As you move a beam of light will descend that will go all the way through you. Keep moving as you accept this.

We are connecting you energetically to all the healing teams from all over the multiverse in this physical Universe and in all the different dimensions. You are connecting into the multiversal agreement between all healers that is purely benevolent.

Accept this connection

Come to stillness in your physical vessel. Put your hands down halfway and feel yourself connecting to all the healers that are surrounding your planet at the moment. Your hands are connecting as you are holding their hands. The many different humans you are connecting in this way and the many different species that are connecting to you, lending their support at this time. Opening up the consciousness of mankind, healing your species completely. Facilitating the eradication of all the negatives that have plagued your society. Bringing you into an understanding of your oneness with your hearts all over the globe. As you embrace all the beings surrounding your planet and all the other human healers they are now raising the vibration in connection and communication with you. You are accepting the multiversal agreement of selflessness and service.

Repeat this statement of intent

I _____ accept my responsibility as a divine healer in selfless connection to all that need help in the evolution of mankind in the transformation of this planet. I connect to all the divine healers in the multiverse of all of creation. I accept and allow all the divine technology from all the different advanced civilisations that I am connecting with now. I accept the flow of the Universe within me now and my purpose to affect healings and to facilitate miracles is upon me. So be it, Amen.

Put your hands back upon your heart chakra and relax in the bliss of the new connections you have made in this physical universe and in all the multiverse that you are now connected to consciously.

Your vessels are changing dear ones. You are becoming more and more sensitive to each other's vibrations. As you open up to the power within you, the healing power, the transformational energy within you you come closer to your source. As you come closer to your source you transform your reality.

This time on the Earth plane is perfect for your transformation. You are ready as a species to take this next leap into your understanding and your cooperation with each other. The old ways you have communicated energetically are dying out. They have to for your survival as a species. The new paradigms of awareness and awakening are being spread far and wide. We are opening you to your conscious healing, your most definite mental understanding. We are connecting you into the frequencies of light that will help your mental telepathy and will help you to heal others mentally. For there are many who are going through self-deception and addiction who are trying to drown out the pain because they are sensitive's. Sensitive to all around them and the societal paradigms that you have put on each other and put yourselves down as being weak. You do not want to show each other how weak you are so in your mental understanding you prove how strong you are through the ingestion of substances and laugh. It is this fear of ridicule and not wanting to be an outcast in your society that has caused many in your species to self-destruct. There are a myriad of different reasons but the main one is the disconnection to your spirit.

As we empower your mental body and tune you into the frequencies of light these things will not affect you anymore, as you will see them for what they are and you will not feed into these deceptions. Not only will this not affect you but you will be able to change the mental frequency of those who need healed and helped and brought onto a more powerful path within themselves.

As a species you are very susceptible to autosuggestion and there are those who take advantage of this to keep you dumbed down to your television sets through giving you false propaganda and helping to keep you asleep. You have had an analogy of this in your film 'The Matrix' which is embedded in your consciousness. Rather than this being a literal understanding of the plot this is an analogy for mankind being hypnotised by mainstream media that is controlled by those who do not have your best interests at heart.

As you are unplugged from this hypnotising you come into an awakening of what is really happening on the Earth plane and at first this may seem overwhelming but this is all perfect dear ones. For the control systems that are in place are being broken down and truth will be sought by each and every one of you who comes out of this trance. And the truth will set you free dear ones.

You are more powerful than you have been led to believe and your ability to heal is much stronger than you have been led to believe also. Even many of your physicians do not understand your healing power as they are being trained to deal with your symptoms instead of the root cause of your problems. The understanding of medicine will take leaps and bounds the more and more of you that awaken and the more that vibrational energy and healing are integrated into your medicinal paradigms.

Do not misunderstand us – the majority of doctors who take your Hippocratic oath are very eager to heal and to help but the majority of that system in its current paradigm is based upon the selling of drugs instead of the understanding of well-being.

This is changing dear ones, as you take responsibility for your own vessels, as you take responsibility for your own vibration, as you take responsibility for your own light. For the majority of your ailments, the majority of your physical symptoms will be dealt with when you awaken and you start to treat your bodies with love and respect. With proper nutrition, with the understanding of Alkalising and hydration, proper breath in meditation and the taking away of stress in connecting into your higher selves.

As divine healers, once you have worked on yourselves this is part of your mission to bring people into their proper understanding of the world and their power.

Exercise will become paramount in your awakened society. And the exercising of your brain waves, of the understanding of what that means and how you can influence others, who are allowing themselves to be in a low vibration, trapped in a sleeping society, controlled subliminally by those who only seek to make a profit will become apparent.

Everything is changing dear ones. The next downloads are to bring you into the vibration of mental calm and will bring you to the point as adepts where you can affect this mental vibration in all that are surrounding you.

Sit in a comfortable position

Regulate your breathing

Accept this download

As we give you this download the grid of mentally connected beings that are of a similar vibration to you will become clearer. The flower of life and its mental vibration is connecting you to all the adepts that are here to awaken humanity. Here to take them out of this collective hypnotism that is not benefitting your society.

This is a mental upgrade

Put your hands over your heart chakra

Accept this download

Be at peace

The fact that you are reading this book and have gotten to this point in the book means that you are of a higher vibration than the majority of humans walking this planet. The more and more people that absorb this information, the more and more lightworkers that walk fully onto this path will join you. For all are love at their core dear ones. You have accessed your love and have an open understanding that something has to be done consciously to bring this planet's vibration to the point where the whole world will heal.

Not all that are reading this book will get to this point for not all are ready for the transformational energies that will bring you into the more multi dimensional awareness that the downloads past this point will facilitate. This has to happen bit-by-bit dear ones so it is not too overwhelming. The gentle flow of love that you will give all will be felt by the most asleep, the most ignorant and even the ones stuck in hatred and violence. Only focus on love always and their understanding will expand.

The downloads from here on in will expand your conscious awareness of the flower of life and your multi dimensional self. Hold your heart chakra as we give you this next download. This will connect you directly into the power of your Sun in this physical universe. As you connect into the power of the Sun you will be greatly energised and your body will begin to vibrate. Do not fear this vibration. This is a very powerful connection. You are grounded into Mother earth and the connection to the Sun will complete the physical connection and allow you to start radiating from your heart the energy of your central Sun. the power of this will change the reactions of people around you as they will feel your warmth and in your presence your radiating light will help heal them. It is important that before you fully absorb this that you fully assimilate the previous downloads as this is a very powerful point in this book and you may find yourself overwhelmed with this power. But after fully absorbing this into your heart centre your healing apprenticeship will be complete and you will move forward as a master.

From this point onwards you will not have any time for anything that does not serve you, for anything that does not serve your highest good and for anything that does not serve your mission here on Earth. Your power will be felt greatly as you embody the Sun. This is what is to be known as a Sun of God.

Embrace this power dear ones

Allow yourself to glow

Allow yourself to embody your divinity

Embrace your power

Accept your divine path

As you fully embrace this download it is all the fuel you need for your merkaba. In this place you can affect complete and immediate divine healing, instant manifestation, bi location, time travel, the power to awaken those who are sleeping and the power to awaken the masters who are waiting to be activated. There are many masters in your society who have not realised who they are yet. The masters are here. You are one of them. You are the Christ, the Christed ones, embracing your divinity. The World merkaba is being activated - you are ready for this.

As the World merkaba opens, the vibration of the Planet naturally raises and the World is brought towards harmony. As this happens all that is not required must drop off. And so it seems as if the chaos intensifies, the fighting, the violence, the manipulation, the greed, and the hunger for power, for domination. It is at this crucial time that those who are here to raise their vibrations and lift all of mankind through this turbulent time awaken from the dust. That time has come.

This is the rapture of mankind that has been spoken of. You must not focus on the chaos, do not subscribe to it. Focus on your individual missions, opening your hearts, being in connection with each other bestowing peace upon those who are ready for this transition and respecting those who have chosen destruction as their path. For Mother Nature does not get it wrong. A flower will only open when it is ready. As you are reading this book you are ready. You are ready to flower. No longer remaining in poverty, accepting your divine inheritance. Walking into your power.

Your Earth is a Spaceship and you were seeded here to pilot it. Your consciousness in connection with each other in your mastery connecting fully with the heartbeat of the Earth will plug you into your divine power completely.

The divine fire is here; it is upon you now and all that are ready for this will synchronise with you. Divine timing is always at work but as you raise your vibration you see the signs of this and you recognise the synchronicities that are here to help you along your pathway. You recognise the people that you are meant to connect with, for there is no such thing as coincidence.

I am raising your vibration; it is akin to flying outside of your atmosphere around your globe. Your physical vehicles have gone through much transition and within a hundred years you will be able to go from one end of your planet to another within a couple of hours. As you break the barrier of the gravity of your planet and you travel outside there is less resistance and your speed multiplies. This will be a regular understanding for you and within your lifetime your engineering prowess will multiply and your technological advances will take your breath away. This in tandem with your spiritual development will bring this World into the Utopia that it was always meant to be and this phase of the experimentation of the expansion of your consciousness will be complete.

This next download we give you is to empty you completely of all resistance and to give you the experience of floating outside of your Earths gravity and giving you mastery over dark gravity.

Once you have fully assimilated this download you will be lighter. And your four-body system will be able to rise unencumbered by gravity. The deeper you go and the more you let go, the more you allow this download the easier it will become for you to levitate in your consciousness and physically. If you bring yourself into the centre point and assimilate this download connecting fully to the zero point of your physical, emotional, mental and spiritual vessel - you must let go of all incredulity and bathe in this light, this lightness of being will physically affect your vessel and will speed up your vibration once again.

Accept this download

Be at peace

Masters of light we give you this as a gift for as you celebrate your birthdays on Earth this too is a celebration. Of you coming of age, of you understanding what you have been given over the ages in your prophetic words. The ones that you have most resonated with, the time is now, rejoice.

The more you let go and the more you empty yourself the more you will be filled by these downloads. These downloads must be taken seriously. Each time you sit in a relaxed and comfortable position, regulate your breathing and allow them to fill you. As you are reading this book you are on a path of truth. The truth towards your real self, your divine self, your expanded self, your glow will be obvious. And as you integrate these downloads more and more you will come to an ease within your life as if you are flying on the outside of the Earth with no resistance. This is the point where the law of attraction is most powerful. Your manifestations become instantaneous and you are able to affect those around you and heal those around you with ease. Many will be drawn to you for your healing power for the affect you have when you are in Peoples Company.

Do not look upon healing as merely healing the physical ailments that you have in your vessels. For you will come to realise more and more that these are all points of experience that you have chosen. Everything that happens within the Earth plane is a choice at some point in your consciousness. The acceptance of this will bring you great ease, will bring you great peace and will centre you into your God self.

The different levels of light that you can assimilate are dependant upon how much you are prepared and ready to let go of all that weighs you down. This expansion of consciousness is what the World has been waiting for. You must start to look at the World as a whole for your species to evolve. No one can be left behind in your consideration. Although they may choose destruction themselves, it is not your place to take this away from them or to reinforce it. Do not help them to their doom instead picture them with an immaculate conception and you will help facilitate their rise in vibration.

This next download is for you to help the leaders of the World let go of their egos and be in their integrity. Seeing them all with an immaculate conception that they may break the shackles of outside economic interests and hold their offices in pure integrity. Wherever you are geographically in the World this is best directed to your closest leader first and then at all leaders so that there will be harmony.

You do not have to be involved in individual issues politically however you will be led by your passion at what it is you are here to fulfil. Always be ready and open to accept that a divine solution will be in your best interest better than one that you feel led by your ego to make a stand for. For all is not always as it seems. There is an organisation that is going on on the Earth plane right now. Do not resist anything for at this point in your vibration it is most important to see the bigger picture and to allow the Angelic influences to do their work. As Masters you are individually responsible for the raising of the vibration and for being in bliss and being in peace which will result in your leaders being given the support to straighten their mental bodies in such a way that they facilitate the transition of this Earth from ego led, power based decision making which is influenced by separate economic interests to that of a pure, transparent and divinely acceptable way of being governed.

Relax and accept this download

Be at peace

Understand that healing comes in many forms dear ones. As Masters you are here to facilitate everything that needs done. Relax and embrace your missions, embrace the peace.

The closer you get to your zero point, to fully assimilating sitting in this place at all times the more your ego will trick you into thinking that you are better or less than others, thinking you are superior or inferior. This is merely a trick for how can you be superior to yourself. All are one and when you are genuinely sitting in your divine centre point, fully in the zero point there will be no thought of superiority or inferiority. You will be in a bubble of truth not influenced by your ego or others egos and the truth of the saying 'Thy will be done' will be complete, for my will and thy will will be one. This is the duality of thinking that will change as you come more and more to the bliss and the peace that passes understanding. For in the saying 'Thy will be done' you are acknowledging an outside source, a higher power. Something that is not in your control that you are giving over your control to God, Spirit, the Universe, however you want to quantify this concept. When you come into your full zero point you will recognise and fully understand and there will be no duality.

Humility is needed for this next download. Surrender, complete surrender to your higher self, to the divine will. This download will expand your power. This download is a very powerful initiation. Only accept this download once you have assimilated all the previous downloads and when you are fully ready to walk into your mastery. Once this download is fully assimilated there will be no need for words. You will find yourself communicating more powerfully, more intentionally with more focus and although you will still speak, brevity will be your friend and you will communicate more fully and completely from your God self. Your experience will be of the fountainhead of bliss. Your physical vessel will be anchored fully.

Accept this download

Breathe in this bliss

Be still

Embrace your I am

I am that I am

There is nothing that is not me

Be at peace

Let go of all attachments. Empty yourself of everything. As you empty yourself you will be filled with spirit. You will be filled with healing. You will be filled with light. You will be filled with bliss. As you do this your personal circumstances will change, will become more fluid and you will embody bliss on a more regular basis. You will be a walking embodiment of light, love and healing.

This book comes at an important time. For the healing of mankind, for the transformation of consciousness that is happening on the Earth plane at the moment. You are blessed to be at the cutting edge of consciousness. You have chosen this. You are more masters than you think.

As you sit in meditation

Picture your Sacral chakra (Below your belly button) connected into your base chakra, connected into Mother Earth.

Picture your Solar plexus (Above your belly button) connected into your heart chakra, connected into your higher three chakras and into Father Sky.

Picture this vividly

Breathe deeply into this vision

Now connect the circuit

From your sacral chakra, below your belly button to your Solar plexus just above your belly button. As this connected point of lightning occurs you will feel electricity flowing through your body.

Breathe deeply into this

Lift your hands in front of you, spread all your fingers, feel the Chi flowing through your body and out through your finger tips

Hold this position

Visualise the point between your Sacral chakra and your Solar plexus very vividly

Picture the lightning bolt between the two points

The more you picture this, the more you feel the chi flowing through you the more you will be energised.

You are now a conductor for healing Chi

Hold your hands in front of you as if you are holding a ball. This is a ball of healing Chi. Energise it still picturing your connection, your lightning bolt between your Sacral chakra and your Solar plexus. You are energising this ball of Chi.

Now picture the recipient of this healing ball of Chi. Picture them within this ball.

Quickly Clap!

You send the energy to them

Hold this ball once again

Now picture the Earth

Quickly Clap!

Picture this ball once again

And picture yourself

Quickly Clap!

Hold your hands out at your side's palms up and picture the lightning bolt between your Sacral Chakra and your Solar plexus.

Come into prayer position

Breathe this energy in deeply

Practice this as often as you can

You are part of the Golden Army of light and as you empty yourself more and more, more and more you will be filled with light. This is an unstoppable force; the time has come for mankind. Embrace your power, embrace your healing, and embrace the lightning force. The time has come.

This book in conjunction with the Clarion call will bring you into a place of complete fulfilment, completely in the moment. As time stands still and you embody the love - all is one. Feel this joy emanating from your heart chakra. We are with you every step of the way and we *are* you. We are your higher self. Have confidence dear ones. For the more you expand your light the easier it becomes.

Do not worry about anything, worry is a wasted energy, It would be better using that energy to take action. Worry only debilitates. Make positive your visualisations and you will be led to where you need to go.

Each individual master that is reading this book has a unique blueprint within themselves for what will bring them their ultimate bliss. For this is the important thing dear ones – that you follow your bliss, that you follow what makes you happy. This will result in the healing of all mankind, the transformation, the ascension. You are conduits of love.

Do not fear anything for this illusion will bend to your will when you come into your power. Seek first to empty yourself, for as you empty yourself of your ego you are filled with your truth. You have much to do.

This next download will connect you into the over seven billion souls that are incarnated on this planet at the moment, all the Animals, all the marine life, all the birds, all the physical life, even the insects and the tiniest minutiae. This is a very powerful download and will expand your empathy for all life and will expand your understanding of who you are and what you are here to achieve.

Relax and embrace this download

Be open and receive

Standing firm as a pillar of light, connecting into the Golden Army, connecting into all levels of your consciousness on your path towards becoming a full embodiment of the divine, an Avatar of light, understanding the blueprint of creation you will be given more and more as the light flows through you. As the Golden power starts to emanate from your heart to all beings you start to operate on the super highway of consciousness. Connected fully to the Galactic council and all that are here to help mankind.

We are going to give you the steps to fully open up your D,N,A. These words are infused with divine purity. Your vessel is a vessel of divine purity.

You are ready for this.

Feel the bliss descending upon you.

Sit in Prayer position

Repeat these words

"I accept the responsibility of my divine heritage. I appreciate all that has gone before and all that is to come and as all strands of my D,N,A are opened I may be fully activated and that all gifts are bestowed upon me. I ask that the Holy Spirit blesses me with all the gifts that are my divine heritage. I claim my inheritance now. I ask that the light of the one flows through me and that all that I say and do from this point forth is in alignment with divine will. I am that I am. I am here to serve. I release this vessel into divine service. Purify and sanctify this vessel. I put all judgement to the side and open to divine intelligence. All that I am, all that I do is in accordance with divine will. Thank you, thank you, thank you, Amen"

You are a Christed being and in understanding what this means you will jump for joy and your energy will transform all that come into contact with you. All that lay eyes upon you will be in darshan and will be transformed. You are the Golden light, you are the love and you will now embody the peace that passes understanding. This will permeate all levels of your being. This is a transformation on all four body systems, mental, emotional, physical and spiritual. Allow the light dear ones. We love you and we are here for you.

This next download is the final download in this book. It is the Chrysalis to Butterfly download. Be brave as you assimilate this download. For this is you coming out of your Chrysalis and emerging as a divine golden Butterfly. Serving the one of all. Be light, allow this energy to flow through you.

Be at peace

Be ready

Be open and receive this download

From this point onwards as you assimilate all these downloads in this book understand that we have put it to you in such a way that you understand that like your computer systems until you have completely downloaded a programme you cannot use it. Therefore this book must be used as a workbook. Over and over for you to sit and assimilate these energies and you will know when you are ready for the final download. You will know when you are ready to embody the bliss. You will know when the healing flows through you. You are ready for this. As a species you are ready but the Masters that are reading this book on the cutting edge of creation within this paradigm are leading the way. You are a blessing to Humanity, coming to this place with your impeccability and your light. You will shine upon others. Be at peace with yourselves dear ones. We love you and we are with you always.

The more reverence you have for yourself, the more reverence you will have for the outside World. And when you realize that all is one and you come together within yourself you will become a server of the light completely. For reverence for self is reverence for God and all that come forward to the light are coming home, you are coming home to yourself. In the beginning of your soul journey you gave yourself a sort of amnesia so you could explore your creation through subjective eyes and as you become whole again you become holy and complete and you see things from the higher perspective.

Respect this book in its brevity. Do the exercises, assimilate the truth of yourself and you will be fit to walk the path of the initiate.

We love you all.

I am Archangel Metatron.

I leave you with the healing book.

18383289R00031

Printed in Poland
by Amazon Fulfillment
Poland Sp. z o.o., Wrocław